ROSA MUNDI

Published by Gunpowder Press
Edited by David Starkey and Chryss Yost
PO Box 60035
Santa Barbara, CA 93160-0035

The publication of *Rosa Mundi* is generously supported by
the Gary and Carolyn Soto Family Charitable Fund

Front cover image by Sarah McCabe

ISBN-13: 978-1-957062-28-0
Library of Congress Control Number: 2026901597

www.gunpowderpress.com

Gunpowder Press is part of Gunpowder Poetry, a 501(c)(3) nonprofit
literary organization

Rosa Mundi

Poems

Mary Ann McFadden

Gunpowder Press • Santa Barbara
2026

For Martha Peyton Kazlo

Contents

IMAGINE

Imagine   3
Morning, Piano (I Can Hear the Wood)   4
The Gentle Man   6
Pantoum for the Orchards of My Childhood   8
Winter of '76   10
Rosa Mundi   15

FUGITIVE

Fugitive   19
Calendars   20
We Walk Through Deep Grass   21
The Tourist: Burma   22
In Croatia   24
Elba: Once and Once Only   25
The Felling   26
Ants Perambulate   27
The Bloom   28
Fast-Moving Clouds   29
Zabriskie Point, Looking West   30
All Desert Sands Are Round   31
A Long Drink of Water   32
McGowan Lake, Summer   33
Spring Water   34

SPEAK

Speak   39

The Pearl Fishers

Les Pêcheurs de Perles	61
Deer at Dawn	62
Among Others	63
The Column	64
All Our Ancestors	65
The Things That Kill Us	66
On Tuttle Creek Road, Thanksgiving Day	67
Bristlecone Pine	68
Flight	69
Change of World	71
Heroes Wake Up in the Morning	74
Thou, Arbiter	76
Night, that Extinguishes My Hand	77
Persimmons	78
That Old Grandeur of the Heart	79
Just Before Sunrise It Begins	80
Swimmer	81

IMAGINE

Imagine

Horses gallop in the dry brush
as dust rises around them, hackberry, scratch grass,
the mountains beyond.

Endless sky on six sides of us.   Wind.

I lift up, tilt along the foothills. I'm old
and I love being old. I'm stiff and sore
just from sitting in a chair.   Imagine.

The straight backs of my friends are learning to bow.
I see stars where the woods were.
Angers and their scars line my gut, and there are days
when they still fester.

I wake up clear, mulling the forms that surge toward me,
that slip like angleworms onto my hook.

I do not know much.   I never know for sure.
I look for what's there, out there, away over the water.

Morning, Piano (I Can Hear the Wood)

In exile, the cellist Pablo Casals began each day at the piano—
Bach resounding from the sun room in Puerto Rico
as Marta set his coffee on the piano shelf.

When Spain was plunged into war, Casals, who had played
his cello for the crowned heads of Europe, hoped
to bring peace to his beloved country. He vowed he would never
perform in public until Franco was gone.

But his gesture had no effect and the violence spread
into all of Europe and much of the world.

My own blue cup. Pianist Glen Gould's towering Bach.
I can hear the wood from deep in the concert grand at Carnegie Hall:

rock hard maple in the action parts, in the wrest-planks and bridges.
I can hear the roots gripped in schist at the melting of the ice age,
the slow rebound of the underlying rock.

Bach, from close-grained, quarter-sawn Sitka spruce—
the same light strong Sitka spruce that lifted over the dunes
in the first airplane.

A friend tunes our piano, an old upright. Three strings together
to ring one note. Felted hammers for eighty-eight keys,
one of them stuck. When we open the lid of the sounding box,
we find a mouse nest, and 30 acorns to grow 30 oaks.

When Casals spoke for peace, he spoke for me, for all of us.

Where are the mouse pups? Where are the pups of the pups?

So today we brought home seventeen more tomato plants.
We must be crazy.

The Gentle Man

Pomona College, 1934.
Dear Folks, I got a letter the other day saying that
I have been accepted at Harvard Business School—
so if I don't go I'll lose the ten dollars application fee.
I rather like the idea of going East for a year—I've
never been very far away from home.

I had six years left unborn
to my life as his child, still deep in my prior life in France on a farm:
I fell down the cellar steps, frightened by a spider
as I reached for a jar of jam.

There was a timeless time of waiting and then I dove, on impulse,

and began to feel the hot press of human flesh again,
and saw through my eyelids the amber light of earth,
and tasted the blood and water of the human gate,

and slid out at last from the rock that held me in its compassionate
core, from the spark where I lived unmeasured, quiet,
poised, awake, not thinking but thought.

Who did the choosing of where and when and with whom?

Like the hens that wander out of the garden into my bedroom,
three of them huddled together, lifting their legs up

and down on the hard floor, necks stretched tall like periscopes,
turning, peering deeply into a world they wanted to know,

thinking "here is where the woman and the cats go,"
but then thinking "maybe not," I followed an insight,

plunged into the dark which came to be a funnel
or an elephant trap: the V of ibis flying North or South.

There's no turning back, think of it, the innocent weight
of each moment. Why aren't we paralyzed by it?

But we don't know, we never know
just where we are in the air of it.

Pantoum for the Orchards of My Childhood

Mother falls asleep with her head on her arm
as bees hang above her mouth, kiss and lift away.
We reach the center of the orchard where the fruit is ripe
& I hear overhead the brisk fluttering of a sparrow.

Bees hang above her mouth, touch, and lift away.
I'm walking, leaping from furrow to furrow.
I hear overhead the brisk fluttering of a sparrow
and the sun is not too hot—It's mid-morning.

I'm walking, leaping from furrow to furrow
pushing aside branches of the the orange trees.
The sun is not too hot—it's mid-morning
as we enter the queendom of bees—they know we're here

pushing aside branches of the orange trees.
They circle, tap, buzz my cheek, my ear
as I enter their queendom, they know I'm here
scratching my arms, sniffing the sour smell of the leaves.

Bees circle, tap, buzz my cheek, my ear.
My aunts walk right through them: I do the same,
scratching my arms, sniffing the sour smell of the leaves.
I feel brave as I watch for stray dogs and skunks.

My aunts are walking right through them, so I do the same.
Granny is in the lead: she begins to sing.
I feel brave as I watch for stray dogs and skunks.
Come, the hive is near. She holds out her hand.

Granny is in the lead. She begins to sing.
My aunts are gathering dark figs, tearing, devouring.
Come, the hive is near. She holds out her hand.
With my small hands I choose the low-growing tangerines.

My aunts are gathering dark figs, tearing, devouring.
Their aprons fill, the weight of the fruit pulls them down.
With my small hands I grasp the low-growing tangerines.
They take their aprons off and make bags of them.

Their aprons fill, the heavy fruit pulls them laughing down.
Bees hang above her mouth, kiss, and lift away.
My aunts take their aprons off and make bags of them.
Mother has fallen asleep with her head on her arm.

Winter of '76

Eight coleus sprawled in plastic pots
set high on two stacked pallets
where windows from the South and West
let warmth fall over them.

I had left my marriage, rented one floor
of a two story house. She had so many plants,
my friend said, and I had a sunny space
where they lived, generous,
as weeks opened and shut, and the winter dark
tipped toward us.

Cedar waxwings filtered south, but the cardinals held,
lit the branch above their nest
while it snowed and kept on snowing.

I put out seeds and suet balls and bowls of water,
hot, so the birds could drink before it froze,
and wrote and studied by their light.

*

My mother had broken and couldn't seem to mend.
There were reasons: we never understood them.
Baulked grief and rage at my father's death,
childhood rape, I'm guessing.

My stepfather weakened and thinned:
cancer killed him, that good man. He was a farmer—
all those pesticides and cigarettes,
but I think he died of sadness.
He had loved my mother since they were young,
and when she married someone else,

he stayed a bachelor, survived the war, waited a year,
and when he knelt, he asked for both of us.
The twins were born and two more kids.
I was the oldest. I had my own room.

Mother heard voices all along, held herself down.
Once we were grown, the glue came loose.
She hid the kitchen knives and all the guns,
walked the railroad tracks at God's command,
starved, sawed the tendons of her ankles and wrists,
and lived on. Locked up, she escaped three times,
swung herself over the concave fence
and walked and lost her shoes and her address.

*

From my mother I learned how much it mattered,
my one life. I took a step, loved a woman who wanted me.
And I began to write, hidden in my car
parked in a woods while my kids were in school.
I pushed the pencil forward, I read wide and deep.
My husband's contempt for me was so great
he wouldn't look at me, walked in at night
and didn't speak, ate the good meals I cooked
and didn't taste them and didn't thank.
I asked him to leave, but I left instead, hoped
for a way forward, a way to take the children with me

*

Six or eight of my younger classmates
sat at my kitchen table, poems rolled and creased
among long loaves of bread, blocks of cheese

and cheap red wine. I had made a hearty soup,
needing to feed them as much as they needed to eat.

We read our poems aloud. Then we read Auden
and Lowell, Plath and Sexton and Elizabeth Bishop.
Someone passed a joint while we took turns
reading Ginsberg"s "Howl." We shouted, we roared,
we tinkled our spoons like Tibetan bells.

And we wept for love, for death, for genius,
and for our own pathetic failures.
Still, we were on the way.
We were on to something big, we knew it for sure.

We read Wallace Stevens, we read Carolyn Kizer's
"Tying One On in Vienna" in our drunkest diction,
and her "Summer Near the River."

She was our teacher. We adored her outrageousness,
her naked voice, the quick tears that wet her face.
We read Kunitz, Roethke, Rilke, Williams, we read Hart Crane:

> *Whitely, while benzine*
> *Rinsings from the moon*
> *Dissolve all but the windows of the mills....*

We read Louise Bogan—all those bright spirits
that joined us in class and trailed us into my kitchen.

We stayed up half the night. They didn't want to go home.
I didn't want them to leave.

                    *

Bill left his folder behind, came again next day.
I was eating lunch, so I made him a sandwich
he ate in two bites. I brought out a pan of flan
I had baked, and we each had a slice.

As we talked, Bill glanced yearningly toward
the rest of the flan. *Go ahead. Help yourself.*
He took smaller slices as the flan shrank,
the pan like a clock and the disappearing day.

With my silver knife he left a last slice so thin
it couldn't stand, but toppled in its syrup.
Oh for God's sake! He made me laugh.

We couldn't get enough of words in their
beautiful shapes, of poems that gave us hope.
He used a fork to mash up the last sweet custardy bits.
After this year, he told me as he washed the plate,
I have to go home to run my father's store.
I'm the only son. There's no escape

                    *

It was the coldest winter of the the century so far.
The Chesapeake Bay froze over.
One of the local families had skated down the Severn River
to eat fried oyster sandwiches at a tavern
near the river's outlet.

                    My kids and I were there
to watch the ships plunge, intrepid, toward the harbor
as ice continents cracked and marbled in their wakes.

The family put on coats and scarves, hats and skates,
pulled the cords tight, tied the knots with frozen fingers.
Mittens went on last. Two of the men had brought hockey sticks
and towed the tired children behind
as they turned upriver.

Rosa Mundi

Clairaudience: a voice out of the air: WARNING:
RED CLOUD APPROACHING THE WEST COAST

My elderly neighbor glares into the distance
shades her eyes with her gloved hand

She's been pruning roses   still holds the shears

All last week her grandson was with her here
they squeezed orange juice   sold it on the sidewalk

She brightens   she turns

Red wave expands toward us

Soundlessly the change   dust

Thank God I wake up   But the ache sticks in my throat for hours
as my fingers assemble themselves over the keys
tap these letters into words into lines into the

still possible utterance   my unsteady heart deep in my chest

my neighbor bending there in her straw sun hat   her
roses yet unbroken on the bush

FUGITIVE

Fugitive

Looking at me close, my daughter told me
You have another twenty years in you, at least.

Now it's ten. And only if she's right.

California winter, not snow and ice, but near freezing at night—
cold that kills the orange blossoms and wilts the coleus.

My old friends are lost in their closets, caught in their fish nets.

My children's father, months younger than I,
cleaned the gutters of his rented house, went to bed
and left his body in the sheets.

What are the things you can hang on hooks?
Aprons, hats. And what is invincible?

Frost on the cabbages, the hole a possum dug in the compost—
that tumbling sink of mushroom stems and garlic husks
gone to greet the Eocene and the protylopus.

Here's an antique postcard in advance: the print depicts
a lake with its cedar stumps. It's spring, and spring voices
drift across the wetlands, sometimes elf light.

Calendars

As kinglets flick through the fence, three of them,
lost in the blossoming bougainvillea—

you plan our year, an act of faith that those days will come,
that bridges will stand,
that we can find our ways to where the calendar says we are going.

Nights, I swing out of my blankets and steady myself.
I listen for your breathing.
The slopes of your body appear to drift.

I've been swept out to sea, and I've been rescued
by a surfer who hated to miss those few waves.
Nobody noticed as I keened out beyond the breakers,
light as a stick. They must have thought I was playing
as I dragged my heavy body onto the sand and turned and wept.

I and I alone. The next breath not arriving, and the next
not arriving—the spirit just beginning to lift.
What's undone will never now be undertaken,
the tart cherries not plucked,
my tongue will never speak another word.
Our calendar thrown away, then,
the most brutal of all our possessions.

Love, I've learned what matters and what won't
as our cells sift into the handsome sheets you chose
as if we were new brides.

You, innocently asleep most nights, and I
measuring the suck of breath, boat, oar, starfish.

We Walk Through Deep Grass

The expensive heart with its gold bonds, with its
Brandenburg Gates all carven. Ornate, horny heart
so heavy to open, so heavy to shut.

Doors of the embassy locked with chains and guards with guns:
your country, mine, who has the passport, who doesn't.

Shoulders back, Soldier: disobey, let them in!
The one throwing her baby over the fence, the one about to be shot,
the one about to be dragged into the stadium basement.

Heart, what is it that sees us?
Hot heart, hurt hart: the gorgeously antlered panting King.

We walk through deep grass closing behind us.
We have all the time in the world.

We arrive, we regard the brittle bush as it—
sun over the sky toward   umbra   nimbus

Heart in bloom, heart of the broken, heart of the hungry
and halt, great hearts, mountainous hearts' abundance
flooding freely: the whole tribe drowned in this canyon.

Harp in the flesh strummed, or bowed upon.
Heart I don't know. Stranger, keep knocking.

The Tourist: Burma

She parts the curtains to look out,
but where they are is not certain. Names drift
over the maps of continents, maps stained with blood,
the ground stained with it
as light comes to the grey skies and waters of the

Ayeryawady River, renamed by the new government,
the General in plain clothes, the capital moved from Amarapura
to Mandalay, and now to Yangon, formerly Rangoon.

The tourist throws on her clothes, her loose straw sandals.
She climbs the stairs to the observation deck.

Somewhere in the boat is the comforting smell of pancakes,
of bacon, of noodle soup.

But what she sees all around is a silence that overwhelms,
it negates: all are erased.

It is here, the mind of God, the body of God, breathing
as the tourist gasps in a kind of free fall.
Particles of sand shift and whisper as the vast delta
accumulates, obliterates.

Last night her stateroom screens were battered and thick
with migrating moths, but the wide, breeding storms of herons
no longer arrive. One of the waiters told her
these jungles were home to many hundreds of elephants
roaming free, but none has survived.

On the dark shore, a woman kindles the first fire:
a thin line of smoke rises slowly westward, drawn by the turning,
the great turning of earth.

On the sandbar where our ship has rested for the night,
a man steps from his slender canoe, walks along the sand
to come close. The tourist boat is dazzling as ships that sailed
into the immaculate bays of the new world— electric lights,
thudding engines churning the silty river water,
pushing away from where he stands.

A clash of pots and pans: breakfast.
The curly bacon drips upon the absorbent toast. Omelets.
Elegantly sliced fruit on a tray.

In the distance, several fires, several trails of smoke.
A canoe breaks from a dark spit, point and boat
joined in a single line: a jot of light, a space opens up
as the boat pulls silently away, and away.

In Croatia

There was a moment—we were in Split—
when five young men sang Croatian folksongs
standing in snowmelt under a bombed-out dome.
We blinked at the sky. Bathtub acoustics: listening and flying.

Three thousand years of Roman stones and Roman bricks,
Corinthian columns still standing, Egyptian lions still obsidian
as song lifted from the o-shaped mouths of the men.

I took a photo of a pietà in Dubrovnik, the man-body of her boy
fallen across Mary's knees. Now Dubrovnik has vanished.

What was it I swore to remember
there in the ringing ruins by clear Adriatic harbors?

What was it I almost knew for certain?

Elba: Once and Once Only

Our companions traveled on toward the mountains
and lakes of northern Italy with our faithful guide, Ilaria:
the restaurants, the art, the weather.

But we had turned toward home, nearing us now
as we toggle in a battered van with its druggy driver.

After the nights of set silver, napkin swans, pillows topped with
chocolates, how quickly my room, clothes unsprung,
resembles a junkyard with its flyspecked trailer.

Here are the Carrara marble rocks I stole, the dead maps,
the musty underpants and bolognese-sauce-smeared shirts, all of it
breathing its last salt breath.
Able was I ere I saw Elba.

Elizabeth mounts the stairs to her rooms above the harbor,
the book of poems I gave her half-read on the table,
zucchini strips garnished with basil, three to a plate.
Lasagna with artichoke, a salad vinaigrette with razor-thin pears.
Fresh-baked tart and coffee. But it was time to fly away,
requited, back to the bus, back to the ship,
over the sea, over the vast cloud cover.

We sped home, hardly a bump on our flight, all day, all night.
And here we are, however, whoever.

The Felling

These words are for the ash tree
that cooled our summer lawns, that stood watch
in the night under star fall and moon ship,

under the whirlpools beyond us, Anemone and Eagle,
under the old constellations, and our own star.

The place where the ash tree stood—a contusion
of upturned earth. For no use, for no reason.

Who are we, walking upright now?

In this haze of gas fumes, by the side of the chemical river,
among armies of children and refugees,
among the spiteful and the willfully ignorant,
among those stifled and numb, I can still hear a grand, heartfelt singing.
Tell me, Love, where is the source of what's best in us,
the listening, flights of the mind, the bone deep drum?

Ants Perambulate

Ants perambulate the coarse mountain sand.
A few turn toward me, smelling the crust
I have in my hand: *Here, you can have some.*
One measures a large corner crumb with its feelers,
Two struggle with a thin strip of basil.
They drag it away, but one is riding on it upside down.
The basil is bent in the shape of the number 7.
It wavers, it floats, it tips this way and that,
teetering towards the ant trail, the cracked cement.

When I was a child, I often played alone. There were many
days like this one—East Wind rattling the thorn trees,
flapping my grandfather's pants on the line.

Today, overhead, the skies are still. Watchful clouds
stay above me for hours, holding, but changing
from walrus to hat-man, to stacks of flattened cakes.
I take sheets and quilts to the laundromat. I whisk
mouse turds from the windowsills and sponge the dried-up stains.
I put clean sheets on the beds and work up a sweat.
Ants cross the flagstones in front of me as I put out sweet water
for the hummingbirds. I watch the number 7 tilt and turn
as I eat the last of my supper. I'm a lucky woman.

The Bloom

The brittle-bush violently shines—a force stilled
above the fluent sand, silvering the roots beneath the sand,
and though it waves along the heated winds
in the hour when fire begets them, it is not reflecting,

no, not from the normal passage of the star,
but up from the plant's own swords.
Sons of the tundra and the grasslands!
Nor is it reluctant to demonstrate
who is master and who is mere.

O absolute chaos of mischief, what muddy dance
can charge the lightning up the rain?
Today the sun does not command. Down here
it is the bloom that takes the sum and center of the day
while the god's obedient horses, not hitched to the chair,
lift their mouths out of the hay.

Fast-Moving Clouds

Shadows smoke down the slopes of Eagle Peak,
fast wind over the sand, over the fleeting pools
where roots of fan palms sink. I put nectar in a glass tube.
I fill the feeder with seed. A parched palo verde
stunts into thicket, haven for snakes
asleep in the look-alike shade and light-patch.
Mirrors glint from afar. Order, disorder—I see it
in my starred hand, scorpion-stung, cracked
as mud in the dry lake bottom, a weakening of cells
and systems, raw shifts and collisions,
a sister sun to the one we fell toward. Collapse:
the dark well and out the other side.
My calamity—this frail lettering a beetle scuffs away.
Stubborn to the end, I make a little piss,
a little wind from my mouth. I hear a small voice—
not even mine, perhaps.

Zabriskie Point, Looking West

Between here and there, Canada geese—disorderly lines
above Death Valley, parents and first-year flyers
learning to coast in the flow of the others.

The three of us wisely take the level path.
We reach for the hand rail, we choose the easy steps.
We have walked from the parking lot to stand and consider.

Zabriskie Point, a peak named for a man, as if a man
were big as all this, as if a man could stride the tectonic plates.

Our elderly aunt is with us as we overlook salt sinks
blasted bare of trees and plants. In the course of her life
she has climbed Mount Whitney and many other mountains.
Unfortunately, they already had names.

Above us, the Sierra Nevada shrug the nations off.
Their granite massif stands clear, and every naked day
their snowy flanks give into rivers.

All Desert Sands Are Round

For Rae, lost to dementia, in her voice.

I forget you, forget place names
like that coastal town with the sidewalk restaurant
where we sat in blankets sipping our pea soup while it snowed.
And oh, the icy air from the harbor
where our grandfathers sailed in wooden ships.

Some days the names blow back to me from their
almost imaginary stations on earth: Dorothy Mae,
who was my mother once,
Straits of Magellan, Cape of Good Hope.

The mountains where my sister and I often walked
let go their avalanche: down quick streams
the blocks of quartz, the metamorphic, the basalts
abrade, knocking their points off as they roll.

Two hundred years rumbling to the sea, where river sand
surges back to the beach, and some of it whips towards the plains.

The corners of my brain have dulled, unfurnished rooms,
those days I was hesitant to tell my love, so far back now,
the slow jam of continent upon continent:
the learned, the unmet, the infinite.

I'm holding to the rail of what might be a flat-bottomed boat
as we plane the broad, brown waters of the Delta—
their burden of sand falling out and out into the Gulf,
extending the land, filling in the low places from the high places.

A Long Drink of Water

A mule sucks water from a trough—the cold stream
snakes up the muscular throat past tongue-wheel, past aqueduct,

and a woman whose years clatter behind her like Crisco cans,
with tiny wild blooms on both sides of her caravan,

while sands flow past date palms and slot machines, and
highway curves incline under the snowy clefts of San Jacinto,

the old woman in this poem drinks from a steel canteen
as if out of the lake itself—her mouth pursed at the

bright-dark surface, dragonflies, pollen glaze in which
she sees a tall girl, coltish, tending toward grace.

She's a long drink of water the woman mutters to herself,
meaning delight, green limbs unfolding, sand waving

into dunes, the coral branch adding a century to itself.
And so her glance stays and stays, slaking her thirst.

McGowan Lake, Summer

In the midst of one of my family's wild conversations
I've walked over here to gaze at the geese. The lake reflects
as they dip their long necks toward pondweed, hyacinth,
and ripples scroll across to the quiet side, the shady side,
towards cedar stumps robed in moss. In my lifetime, the trunks
have swollen and softened into tiny islands where, at night
the water birds rest. It's just after breakfast as the talk
unspools without me, roars of laughter and argument,
the quieting when someone speaks about her work.
All the new thinking, the confidence that their lives will go on,
the joyful planting of orchards, the love of animals, and of each other.

Tom and Eric talk fishing for hours. *It's almost*, they grin,
better than the fishing itself. Both are happily limping
from a slide down a mountain bank to fish the pockets—
the inaccessible stream with its fat rainbows caught and released.

In one photo, Tom's square hand is clamped firmly around a trout.
The hook has been tenderly removed. It is the moment
just before the fish is lowered back into the stream.
What does it promise us, this fish, stunned as if asleep,
breathing water again, the quick flash, the amazed re-entering?

Spring Water

From snowmelt it flows through an old iron pipe
alongside the trail. When I arrive, in May,
the water comes so hot I have to fill the pool at night.

Bees feed on the yellow blooms. Hummingbirds
buzz the empty feeders: I'll fill them tomorrow, first light.

The heat of us in the winter sun, the craving.
Books, conversations underlaid with gold,
our young bodies learning themselves, learning each other.
A burn in the lips and in the hands, the heart all rattled and galloping.

Now the water slowly wets the cement, overruns the pond.
Sticks and petals turn smoothly toward the overflow
as water spills to the culvert beneath the lower road.
I should turn it off, and I will, soon.

And now I've, against all my fears, married again.
Not easy to keep from drowning. I can love and breathe.

*

Outside, in the dark, a fox glides past: she's avid,
she does not veer. She bores down the canyon
toward the night kingdom where the voles play.
She's healthy and hungry: she will kill.

*

This was a day in which almost nothing happened.
I've eaten a very good cheese sandwich, I've drunk six glasses

of water, which isn't enough. I've written these words.
I've reread some pages of Robert Hass, his Collected.
I took a brief nap and woke myself snoring.

The pool filled with tepid water, fresh from the spring.
I showered. I peeled and ate an orange.
And ate the chocolate cookies. All of them.

The unspeakable fullness of those days—the overfilled cup,
the poise of it. My unaccustomed heart.
Now we hardly ever speak, each lost in her long life.
You were always busier than I, as—I admit it—most people are.
Idleness is my metier, watching as the words shift in their pupae-skins.
Of course I don't regret those times—not a jot, never, not an instant.

A friend arrives, a much younger woman—
full of bright conversation and humor, yet she struggles
with depression, wonders if she drinks too much,
writes poems that slay and resurrect.

We swim that day and the next. She's naked. Lovely.
I watch her dive and surface until, after lunch, she packs her car
and drives down the steep road, and north.

                    *

I work down the familiar list, sweep and mop the floors,
lock the windows and smooth the bedcovers flat.

I check the hooks on the screen doors and hope no mouse
has slipped in to starve during my absence.
Goodbye until the fall.

                              *

I'm writing these last lines at home, home to another season—
our calendars scribbled in pencil and ink, our bodies thick
with all we've lived, the little we regret—
and this customary, singular happiness, sweet
against time, and still sweet against reason.

Speak

Speak

We were passing through the town where I had lived a long time ago,
driving the old road through the orchards.
Two deer stepped away from what had been a children's park,
the road now closed, cracked, overgrown.

The deer had been about to enter

I swing too high,
I slip off into the air
my legs are still bent
to the shape of the swing seat
my arms whirl backwards to keep myself upright
I can see the whole church picnic
deviled eggs   devil's food cake
if my mother sees me   my flight   my mistake
my dumb bumble-bee

but when we stopped, they turned:

first the stag with his tall antlers stood and considered,
as if holding perfectly still would prevent us from seeing him,
yet seeing us. He felt our glances pass him, he leapt to the side
of the road, leapt over the fence and back into the shadows.
The doe, who had already entered the old park, turned and stood,
rooted, looking at what we were, then leapt to the fence,
struggled through, jumped away into the woods.

I stand at the edge of formlessness with my desire—

the deep dark, the close, the distant,

the dream of love, the actual presence of love.

Particles blast from a milkweed plant: everywhere, and up.

Magnetic fields: impeccable arrows straight by sunlight.

One mile high, monarch butterfly smells its one food.

One painting
more than the others, summons me.

I see it on the wall. It sees me standing winter and summer.

I see my one food a mile away. I see the mind, I see the brushstrokes,
I see the hand and body of the one who made this.

I see her little campfire. Hello, hello.

Once upon a time
I was closing the desert house.
I put out a rank piece of meat I hadn't cooked,
set it on a boulder twenty yards out.

The flies came first, one and then others
circling in excited thirst.

From out of an empty sky the hawk surprised us.

Even after the flesh was taken, the rock held a stain
and the flies dotted it up with their mouth-parts.

Once upon a time

we were crossing Puget Sound on a ferry,
lost among the stormy shoals of rain one January.

We plunged into a sunny clearing, a sanctuary

where the light was glancing in a holy way.

A single, small cloud played by itself, and proud, began to snow.

Seagulls flew in and out of the light and the shadow.
A whale, Orca, arose from the icy waters

and everything else fell away. Only this presence, this wilderness
that seemed not to see us, seemed not to care.

Perhaps it saw us as something out there sees us,
but it was not for us:

it was for itself.

In the trunk of my car, in a cardboard box
was a dead cat.
We were taking it to the island to be buried.

I was stoned, as I often was in those days,
wanting another world, wanting to be elsewhere,

though I adored my children, little anchors to the life I led,
the only world I had, the one I have now, the only world.

My two passengers had met in the army.
They were kicked out for loving each other.

Two women intimately touching
in a motel room off the base, arrested and interrogated
separately, broken down until each betrayed the other.

This cat was their child. They were grieving so deeply
I couldn't take it in, couldn't bear the cargo of grief they carried.

For me it was a field trip, a boat ride.

What did I know?

What did I know?

I was always falling.   I'm falling now.

Darkness, teeming and fluent, dynamic, in abeyance.
A wall is holding the flood away.

A belief is holding it away.

I know the fish are there. They must be. I picture them
shimmering below the clear moss-green screen of water.

Shadows, eggs, scales, we smell them,
we remember them jumping far off in the late afternoon.

But here is something I've not seen.
I don't know what it is.

It was not always there waiting for me to discover it
like a species of plant flowering in Brazil.

No, it was not anywhere.

I create it by my longing and by my pursuit:

flesh and bone, grey matter, electrons racing around the track
with their necks stretched out,
their numbers, their mechanical rabbit ever elusive,

but they can smell the blood.

A friend who takes bad pictures of me
claims the camera takes what's there. But she clicks the shutter
when what she wants to see comes clear.

Unconsciously she chooses

among the many little movements and moments.

It's also true
that I do not give myself to her lens,
that I hide myself from her and from others.

You have to catch me unaware.

A gift in a box, wrapped and tied with strong string.
I lift it, hmm, I shake it:
does it slide, does it rattle?

What do I want the gift to be?

What are you so close beside me?

I fondly remember the worst birthday gift:
home-made underpants sewn from flour sacks, edged
with faded rick-rack.

It was a torture device, an itch-cloth on my tender legs and crotch.

Better she not start scratching those parts,
my mother thought, but didn't say,
as she tossed them out.

The metaphor, the stone and flint, the spark.

The dream I want so much I don't let it form in my mind.

Better to not want than to be disappointed,

better to not want than to be shamed, revealed in my longing.

Do we catch it from the air?

Is it a wind that blows through us?

Are the dead, the not yet born speaking through us?

Is the earth speaking through us?

I always wanted to be able to fly.
But I wouldn't trade flight for speech.

Like an upsurge of snow geese—clattering thrill of connection,
my voice flies out of me into music, human music.

Friends come bearing oranges and laughter.
I had set aside this time. But they knock, they call.

Remember how greedy we were when we were young?
There was never enough to satisfy our longing.

Tonight, again, we croon over our table.

We bite down.

My neighbor opens her door in the morning dark.
Her little dog runs out and is whisked away in an instant.

Coyotes, we say, and though the coyote is not large,

it seems large in retrospect.

The loss was large,
her companion, her little pet.

We long for the endless, for where we came from,
the door unopened.

We long for where we are going.

Look back. Look ahead.
It tears us apart. It remakes us.

The sperm springs for its life.

The cow jumps over the moon.

I go with them to the ultrasound—think of it:
sound that makes a picture, that defines
what was finally there in the dark.

I'm afraid to see it.

What if it looks like a lizard or some not-human thing?

And there she is, eyes shut, waiting,
waiting in grace—

plump cheeks, huge hands, legs that fold, little buddha,
little woman in time.

It's there, the new shape of our human heart—

54

I want this. I longed for these
infinitely far and infinitely fair sparks.

I don't know why it seems to me like justice.

*fair: of wind: not excessive; favorable for a ship's passage—
promising good fortune, auspicious.*

just: so as to fit exactly, righteous, equitable.

I can see the trace of a future self who walks toward me:

We touch in a mirror, breathe each other's breath.

We speak.

And the sound of it—deep tones in our throats,

cellos instead of violins. We know.

We know who and what we have become.

The sail in us in not set,

not bellied forth fully as in our youth.

But we still respond to the wind touch

as paper responds to quill

and speaks words never thought of.

This new world.

This sinking, burning land still holds us up.

Temperatures rising all around the planet:

floods, storms, quakes, waves, winds,

trees tumbling down, even the oldest, wisest ones.

We watch ourselves become lumber: a boat, a door,
a splinter, a fire.

Breathe, the heart's hard command.

Love. Love your life. Love your neighbor,
your mate, your stranger.

Love your devils, your hunger,
your fears, your pain.

Turn, and and turn again.

THE PEARL FISHERS

Les Pêcheurs de Perles

—the opera by Georges Bizet

Illusion for the first scene:

In their harnesses, suspended behind a blue scrim, dancers
appear to swim down, dragging their clouds of bubbles behind them,
and slowly swim back up.

I'm breathless. I know where I am. I know what day it is,
what year—though for my body, each day is a smaller fraction
of the life already lived. At birth, an hour is all of it: mouth-search,
sleep, being lifted and being set down. Momentous hunger,
satisfaction, the breast like a god for you to take.

26,000 days and still the dawn delights, haze of fog above the river.

26,001 sequins shimmer on my skin, my costumes
are hung in my star closet, I can dive down, I can find
the embroidered jacket, marble, lint, and acorn

lodged in its pocket, and I can find my teacher with her roll of tape.
This is how to make a cardboard pueblo.
There's my little hand holding my paintbrush, waiting my turn.

Today, and today, and today.
To be human: the achievement, the redemption.

Les Pêcheurs de Perles—its first production at the Met in a century,
tenor and baritone lying about friendship, the spectacle,
the lucky pearl, the kindness returned.

Deer at Dawn

I can measure the coming of the light
by their shapes appearing. Entirely still.
Of the same substance as the air and the field.
Gradually apparent, cut out from the pale greens and grays.

Molecules of water, prisms break into fawn
and doe, dawn and foe

and red fox and hedgehog and junco.

Registration of light upon light: waves surge toward me
as I watch them fly apart from their infinitely small centers.
Shards enter my mouth, my hair, until finally

I can see their jaws grind steadily, like machines.

The one nearest to the woods lifts her tail and shakes it,
lifts her head to look around, lowers it to keep on passing sedge,
sandwort through herself and back to the grasses again,

steaming pellets full of seeds and bodily acids, dense, dry,
drop to the ground, not lost but transformed,
every blade of bitter cress, every soldier, every son.

Among Others

Already a breeze has come down from the north
where farmers harvest beans and wheat—
the rich ones in air-conditioned combines, the poor ones
who pick by hand. When this north wind freshens them,
they stop and shout to each other.

Next months' storms will bring geese and grebes overhead,
and the winds after that will bring ice and snow.

So many choices we have to make, so many ways to go wrong.
Around us is suffering we don't know how to change
and in our cities, even in our warm coats we shiver.

When a gulf of cold air pours a thousand miles across the earth
and ruffles us, we are glad we live among others.

Though even the smallest act of kindness can turn out the wrong way—
a dollar placed in the outstretched hand
can come to the price of a meal or a drug, the words we mean to say
can be misunderstood, and love, that glimpse of good, can sour.

Though every righteous place we construct together can slip
and destroy, we can hide our heads in one another.

What we need is somewhere out ahead of us.
What we want is just to see one thing clear.

The Column

Up where the entablature
widens to the architrave,
below that, on a shelf,
a pigeon is hunched, its
shrill feet spread flat, its
head under its wing.
It has eaten a plastic bag,
and can't un-swallow it.
It kept taking it in and in,
and now the bag is
coming out of its rectum,
and down the length of the
bag blood is dripping.
The pigeon has pulled at the
bag to try to get it out, pale bag
and pale gut twisted so each tug
pulls the body apart, pulls
the heart, pulls the life undone.
To eat again without suffering.
To fly without this dragging flag.
I call the building superintendent.
His name is John. He brings a ladder
and lifts the pigeon down, and snaps
its neck and lays it, limp, on a pile
of new-cut grass in the trash bin.

John leads me into his kitchen
and makes coffee. He talks about
his time in prison, the torture,
the unendurable now long past, his
pretty wife, the boy and girl at school,
his life now in America, not quite
what he had hoped, but so much better
than what he lived before, what his
parents lived, god rest their souls.

All Our Ancestors

I crawl out of my tent onto the sand.
Four giant figures stand against the night skies.
I walk toward them, lean into them, warmed, embraced
as the night around us turns. Our old friends the dippers,
Andromeda, Orion, Gemini, the Good North Star.

Ancestors, plankton swimming there.

I look down, when I dare. Phosphorescent waves
bounce toward us, voracious rush of particles,
salt breath collapsed, bleating, alive, then gone.

    1910. Halley's Comet appears. My grandmother, Dorothy,
    is twelve years old. She counts the years ahead.
    If she lives to be eighty-seven, she will see it again.

But she dies at eighty-two. Three of us gather in the desert,
Aunt Rae, Aunt Merilie, and me. Mother is in the asylum.
We set our clocks for two a.m. when the comet will appear
over the high San Gabriels. I wake my children. They stumble
over the rocks and scorpions to see the dim blur.

Three nights we invoke her presence, Dorothy, Gift of God,
all our ancestors flowing in the dark, in the windy days,
in the ice cold spring, in the movements
of our hands and the set of our chins.

The Things That Kill Us

When we decided to finally put the old dog down,
she had pooped in the house for months

and got lost in her own yard, or on the rocky beach
at dusk, too deaf to hear us call.

She only knew to stand, shivering,
waiting for what would take her: the incoming tide,
the gang of raccoons, rats squealing in the culvert.

And then she saw us climbing toward her.
She knew we would come.

I had named her for my enemy, as if to insult
my enemy, but she became an emblem
of forgiveness: the enemy invited in, brushed free
of burrs, trusting us for food, for praise.

When it was time, she lay down where I asked her,
gave her assent as the needle went in.
The kind Mexican doctor spoke low, wept with us.

She showed me self-compassion: she was never ashamed.
I miss her as I walk toward my old age, my forgetting.

On Tuttle Creek Road, Thanksgiving Day

We passed a dozen steers in a field of snow.
They had gathered to eat fresh hay spread on the ice,
green alfalfa packed in bales and flaked into thick cakes.

Each winter morning the man and his boy lift it down
from the truck and rake it out. The steers chew and swallow,
their four stomachs digest even the weeds that horses can't eat.
Their jaws rotate slowly. Their molars grind and their juices flow.

When dairy cows are loosed from a winter barn on the first
warm day of spring, they leap and twist and their udders swing like clouds
—only women in the fields that day. No business
with the bull, just grey-pink tits and buds of blue clover.

These are black angus, castrated males, just boys, really, raised
for their meat. Around them, snow is heaped on the fenceposts.
Canyons deep, avalanche poised on the far slope.
The herd huddled together in the dark. They lay down
to protect their bellies, stayed down all night.

Now they get up. Crusts of snow slide off their level backs.
They scrape with their hooves, they gather together
at the place where their feed is spread so that everyone can eat.
So that everyone here can eat.

Bristlecone Pine

Her sprout broke the glacial ice, held
where few beasts could reach her.

Five thousand years passed.
Soft skies whiffed. Seasons snapped.

Pyramids, civilizations hopped and skipped.
Vast armies sparked. And yet

the life in her pressed, and still the thick sap
urges upward in a single living strip of bark.

She stands. Anchored in adamant.
The eons in her wood arrest.

Her years ring thinner than the thinnest paper.

She stood at the making of our clay tablets
and stands now at the end of books.

Flight

So it happens.
So a way opens for us.

The body, which is also the mind, will not lie to us,
even though we urge it on with whips and oxen, we can tease it,
hurry it, make it perform, but the body will not fly until it happens.

"It's so luxurious!" someone cries crushable in my arms
as what is most unfettered in us joins and rejoins.

All my life I've seen migrations of birds veer together as one mind.
Here we are, alive, the way open for us.

South and North, Summer and Spring, the gift of physical love,
the mind preened to the fingertips, the mind's mouths kissed,
the mind's speechless sunsets and forbidden cities.

All my life. What else might be possible, if love like this is possible?
Even for a moment?

Years have passed. It still exists, the gift of physical love:
the way I failed to dominate with my heart and my rushing words,
the way I learned to trust your intelligence.

It existed once, it still exists, I believe in it the way I believe
it happens, a way opens to us.

Our private, complicated lives, our graceful choices,
always, now, in light of this physical love,

what it has meant to us, what everything else means,
how even though the heart can change,
I love, I have been loved,

the body can turn away,
it exists, it happens.

Change of World

Tomato, strawberry, sweet corn, peach.

In the migrant camps and in the streets,
mothers sell themselves for a dollar.

Men in black cars take orphans for slaves.
Nobody stops them.

A four-year-old girl with blood between her thighs
is unable to speak. A boy has seen too much:
something's wrong with his eyes.

Some speak low, they teach, they examine the stars.
They kneel beside the wounded, they carry their young
on their backs and in their arms.

Blackberries, figs, honey trees that thrash and release.
Among roses, between thrown-back sheets
your mouth is a wing, my breast is another wing.

*

The armadillos are walking slowly north
on their tough little feet. Refugees push past borders.
learn new languages, new foods to eat.
I can pack my backpack. I can wear my sturdy shoes
and follow the faint prints of the armadillo
if I can find the trail.

Desert heat: the animals begin to suffer.
Immaculate colts of sandhill cranes, cattails

wither in the slough, grackles
chatter from wires and fenceposts.

Does the armadillo make it to a burrowing place
along a shallow northern river?
Do the offshore islands blaze across the sky?
Does the towering wave crash over us?

Do they find me petrified in sandstone,
surfing with my arms out, or in a peat bog preserved
with buttercups in my mouth?

After the quake, the fires, mayhem,
the faithful drowned with their choirs, after the virus
and the cure, the starving-out of the poor again,
what do the dazed habitants make
from the heaps and shards?

*

The sea otter had the softest hair, more than any animal,
a million hairs per square inch—so much hair

she didn't need blubber for warmth.
She anchored her cub in seaweed, she tended and fluffed,
warmed herself in the sun before she
dove deep in cold water.

*

"Otter" rhymes with "water" in English,
but does it mean that these shapes
sparked from our tongues?

I don't under-estimate language, or prayer—
those most mysterious, most supple.

What words, what longing calls the otter?

Rhythm and rhyme.
Song of the cricket repeats, repeats.

Heroes Wake Up in the Morning

for Bill McKibben

First light. All the plants are happy in their pots.
Still very quiet.

His love's asleep in their bed for once. Not up before him.
The boy's asleep. A sleeping world—

Yesterday gnarled into a messy pile of string.
Another march today, another confrontation, letters,
interviews—

       All the spirits wake pure,
the spirits wash their human hands and faces,
some bathe their whole bodies for the pleasure of water,
the clean between the legs, the toes, the hair.

Under the nails, behind the ears, the armpits, neck and chest.

They bend down to scrub feet refreshed now after standing for hours
in the sun, after walking and shouting, after kneeling
to paint the words that might speak to someone—

not forgetting the eyes, corners of the eyes, the crusts of sleep
carefully washed away, the dreams, the dogs, the plastic
handcuffs, the heads beneath the clubs—

the armored, the booted, the helmeted,
the vulnerable, breathing plates of the skull above the brain.

The man sleeps soundly, sleeps exhausted, sleeps in his loose,
cool clothing.

                    The woman sleeps deeply, and deeply dreams.
She's counting the last seventy elephants as they go down.

She's counting clouds, counting club cars, counting cabooses,
counting cakes, counting heads in baskets, counting cups of cream.

From time to time, she turns over, lifts toward morning,
falls back again. From time to time the dream drifts toward him
and he seizes it like a cup of coffee in his two hands.

The dream enters him and rolls him over underneath the tank of it,
a voice is screaming, many voices, but he understands their
language now and runs toward them.

Children watch their mothers hang clothes among the ruins,
fathers shout, older brothers gone away, the drone
clicks high and invisible, the steel brain, the lethal load
simmering dark, the dumb elements, tar, powder, chromium—

The mockingbird scolds the cat outside in the coming light,
the hero wakes again. His love breathes beside him.

He begins to think of the day ahead: where is it going,
this endless work? He lets that thought fall away,

mutters again the words he wakes with:

"Not for myself. Not for myself,"
words a strong friend gave him to say.

Thou, Arbiter

Where will we run, without houses?
What will they shout, the broken, the disarranged,
those thwarted and blocked, the terrorized, those in childbirth,
those in a ditch, who changed their minds, with closed fists,
who were tampered with, the speechless, the smeared,
those buried half-alive, those who live without animals,
who chop down trees, the cursed, the artless.

What will become of the mourners, those with emerald rings,
or sitting sad in cafes, the ones who wish to be dolphins.

All that time preparing ourselves. And when we are sucked
into the dust-bin with everyone we love
and everyone we hate and all their kin, with elephants
shot for their tusks, sows with their piglets,
the jubilant, the generous—O Sly Order and Force,

what of all the candles we lit? Moon-tongue, Fountain,
Brothel of cowbird and fox, ink and papyrus, Thou, Arbiter
of wolves, cranes, crows and yarrow, may the mountains yet harbor
the marmoset, may the condor loop once more over the bus.

Night, that Extinguishes My Hand

When I blow out the lamp
and my bed knocks softly on the wall,
and the vertical lines of the bookshelf, chairs like upright citizens,
windows like paintings I daubed with my brush and framed—imaginary
animals running, and their shadows running beneath them—

I pray that these objects are here intact, that these ties hold
even in the pull of our one moon. I reach out my hand,
my left hand, for who can sail without a map?
My ships, O Magellan, my pajamas hung on a hook,
where did their sleeper go?

Night, that extinguishes my hand, and every thing my hand
has made, you windows plowed from the wall,
show me now what you showed before! You, black wind,
harbinger and dart, with the intricate thistle of your tongue,
among lies and lords, along tarred floors,

pants unbuttoned, among bread crumbs, molecules and homonyms,
keep me, whisk me past hooting owls,
hum of hive-wings warming, cooling, trove of infant spiders
swinging in the elbow of an arm, oh my tissue, bone-flake,
my old milk, my verb, pulse and spark.

Persimmons

When the gods clap their boots together now,
crickets rain on our porch, and cherishments
rattle in our valentines, intelligible somehow.
And these are not the best of our embarassments,

daft among brambles, merry in mayhem.
Tonight we pick the bright persimmons
that ripen in time for what we make of them.
Dry leaf that crowns the lucid flesh: ignite!

We know nothing of each other. What
can we absolve in the time left? How much
can we accept? As flocks, as fields, as choirs—
one fruit, the most ravishing, is ours.

What the heart wants, the heart provides.
But what love this is, love decides.

That Old Grandeur of the Heart

We roll on into the year, miss the pot-holes, pay the rent.
North of here, a single blackened house stands on the hill.

One family who lost everything, everything they owned,
shelters in a cheap hotel. The children, phoneless,
sit with their parents to talk. One asks: what can we do to help?

In a way, their mom says, we've never been happier.

Among earthquakes, hurricanes, or in the heat
that's begun to swell the oceans and overcome the coastlines,
some of us will have a chance.

Among plagues, at the hills of dead geese, among the starved,
the ungenerous, there will be those who share, who teach.

Poetry will not die. A thousand years from now, we will parse
our myth—that we drummed among the scrub,
that new forms intrigued us, that we held
to our botched migrations.

With our cracked hands we sought the moist, fragrant places.
In our cloud beds, our pods, our vast, glassine cities,
we will rock ourselves. We will still find one another.

Just Before Sunrise It Begins

The infant cottontail slips from the doe's birth opening
and burrows into the fur-lined nest.

It is the quietest speech,
this blurt of steaming, fragrant skin alert to the cold.

Eyes shut tight, nostrils open
as her mother comes close to let her nurse.

A world floods her brain, smoke on the mountain,
wiggling baby animals within the hill.

Chilled air seeps into the dens, gasses rise in plumes
above burdock, clover, stinkweed, thistle.

Unaccountable, the new year.

Fresh tracks on the sand:
badger with his pigeon-toed diagonal walk
crossed the alluvial slope, stopped, sniffed, veered
around clumps of mesquite and creosote.

Swimmer

Among the heavens and the creatures we leaned, barefoot
on a beach so wide, so swift the surfaces hurled us
out of the thoughts we wished to think, as waves thumped
around us, and spiders spun us into wide, white spires.
Nations flew upon their pillows, dove among starfish, twinkling
insects, plankton brilliant black in the skies, and all of it
held us within it, alarmed, beating our breasts with our fists
flare after flare, and soldiers of the king fired rockets, feared
our convulsions, startled salts bursting in air, O mothers and fathers,

your bare lineaments and seams, garments around you like silicone
silk, milk of conception, egg and wagging stick. Our mothers
and fathers the bare lineaments and seams of garments
around you like silicone silk, your pursed lips blow us across.
Salt of us drowned, daring. Do you feel the pull, O diviners,
among chiton-starred backs of sand crabs, the yearn of our hands
and your hands to meet beneath our chalk? More than matter
for we love our human horse, nostril breath blown quick,
clay brushed from a sleeve, eyelash. Each new wave
crashed past us onto the waking self, sun-span, ocean path.

Breaststroke, frog kick, flutter flutter feet. Breaststroke,
frog kick, flutter flutter feet. Reach and reach and breathe.

Acknowledgements

My thanks to the editors of the following publications in which these poems first appeared.

Apercus Quarterly: "The Column" and "Night That Extinguished My Hand"

Askew: "A Long Drink of Water"

Hanging Loose: "Imagine" and "Rosa Mundi"

Solo Voyage: "Persimmons" and "The Gentle Man"

Spillway: "Bristlecone Pine"

"Imagine" was also anthologized in *Women in a Golden State: California Poets at 60 and Beyond* (Gunpowder Press, 2025).

Gratitude and Appreciation

Thanks to my family: Tom Wilson, Dorothy Leland, Carolyn McCabe, and my dear cousins, Charlie and Renee, Mike, Curtis and Marilyn, fellow poet, to Jerry Robertson and Colleen, to Danny and Cathy Robertson, and to my wave-riding buddy Terry Ince, and to my last living Auntie, Merilie Robertson, going strong at 97, and to her older sister, Rae Wilken, who is gone but very much not forgotten. Thanks to my cousin Glen Rasmussen and to Marilyn.

Thanks to Kathleen Bishop, my Beloved. Among so many other things, she gives me a lovely place in which to live, and drives me most days since she thinks I'm a menace on the highways. Thanks to my grown children Geoff McCabe and Sarah McCabe for being so kind to me, even after their tortured childhood which they love to recount. (Mom to kids: I'm writing. Do Not Disturb me for ANY REASON. Unless there's blood.)

Thanks to my friends for making me laugh, for keeping me company. To the largehearted Martha Kazlo, to dear Anne Lewis, to Joan Larkin, whose poems continue to teach me. To the poet Judy Oberlander for so many years of friendship, and to Lynne Wetzell. Thanks to Joy Manesiotis, Jennifer Sweeney, and Youna Kwak for their brilliant advice and generous readings of my work. And for their own work that inspires me.

Thanks, wordless thanks to two friends who have passed from the earth but not from my heart, Patricia Forsberg and Leslie Hall Pinder. I can't believe you're gone. I can't stand it that you're gone.

Thanks to the members of the Ventura Arts Council for their support during my laureateship, and for excellent friendship: Phil Taggart, Marsha de la O, Anita McLaughlin, Mary Kay Rummel, Friday Gretchen, Sean Coletti. And to the very excellent poet David Oliveira, so far away but so close. Thanks so much to the brilliant Lisa Coffman. Thank you to my editors at Gunpowder Press, Chryss Yost and David Starkey. Thanks to Sarah McCabe for her stunning art work.

Thanks to my parents and grandparents. Thanks to my life.

Mary Ann McFadden is the current Ventura County Poet Laureate. Her first book, *Eye of the Blackbird*, won the Four Way Books Intro Prize in Poetry, 1995. Her second book, *Devil, Dear*, was published by Alice James Books in 2014. She has been published in a range of journals, including *Southern Poetry Review*, *Kayak*, *The American Voice*, *Nimrod*, *Bloom*, *Green Mountains Review*, and *Psychology Tomorrow*. Her poems have been anthologized and nominated for a Pushcart Prize. In 2010 she was awarded a MacDowell Fellowship and spent six glorious weeks among the musicians and painters and writers there. Her first great teacher was Carolyn Kizer, who tutored her on Stanley Kunitz and Theodore Roethke, especially. She received her MFA from NYU where her teachers were Galway Kinnell, Sharon Olds, and Yehuda Amichai, among others. In 2005, she had several poems set to music and performed at Carnegie Hall.

BARRY SPACKS POETRY PRIZE

Color Advisory Board, poems by Michele Santamaria
Dear Empire, poems by Holly Karapetkova
Burial Fragments, poems by Keith Ekiss
In the Cathedral of My Undoing, poems by Kellam Ayres
Accidental Garden, poems by Catherine Esposito Prescott
Like All Light, poems by Todd Copeland
Curriculum, poems by Meghan Dunn
Drinking with O'Hara, poems by Glenn Freeman
The Ghosts of Lost Animals, poems by Michelle Bonczek Evory
Posthumous Noon, poems by Aaron Baker
Burning Down Disneyland, poems by Kurt Olsson
Instead of Sadness, poems by Catherine Abbey Hodges

DRYDEN-VREELAND BOOK PRIZE

Lung Hours, poems by Jessica Purdy
Night Halves, poems by Christine Marshall
Three-Day Weekend, poems by Christopher Blackman

ALTA CALIFORNIA CHAPBOOKS

Patrilineation, poems by Carlos Andrés Gómez
Here, on this 76L, poems by Michelle Moncayo
Alba and Other Songs, poems by Fred Arroyo
The First Amelia, poems by Amelia Rodriguez
On Display, poems by Gabriel Ibarra
Sor Juana, poems by Florencia Milito
Levitations, poems by Nicholas Reiner
Grief Logic, poems by Crystal AC Salas